STOKELY
CARMICHAEL

and Black Power

by Robert Cwiklik

GATEWAY CIVIL RIGHTS
THE MILLBROOK PRESS
BROOKFIELD, CONNECTICUT

Photographs courtesy of: © Flip Schulke: cover and cover
inset, p. 4; UPI/ Bettmann Newsphotos: pp. 1, 2–3, 9, 10,
12, 15, 22, 27; Bonnie Freer/ Photo Researchers: p. 6; AP/
Wide World: pp. 17, 18, 21, 24, 25, 26, 28, 29, 30.

Library of Congress Cataloging-in-Publication Data
Cwiklik, Robert.
Stokely Carmichael and Black power / by Robert Cwiklik.
p.   cm. — (Gateway civil rights)
Includes bibliographical references and index.
Summary: Describes the life and accomplishments of the civil
rights worker who took a controversial, aggressive stance in his
struggle for black rights in the 1960s.
ISBN: 0-395-67002-0 (pbk.)
1. Carmichael, Stokely—Juvenile literature.   2. Afro-Americans—
Biography—Juvenile literature.   3. Civil rights movements—United
States—Biography—Juvenile literature.   4. Civil rights workers—
United States—Biography—Juvenile literature.   5. Black power—
United States—Juvenile literature.   6. Afro-Americans—Civil rights
—Juvenile literature. [1. Carmichael, Stokely.   2. Civil rights
workers.   3. Afro-Americans—Biography.   4. Afro-Americans—
Civil rights.   5. Civil rights movements—History.   6. Race
relations.] I. Title.   II. Series.
E185.97.C27095   1993   973'.049607302—dc20
[B]   92-11560   CIP   AC

Published by The Millbrook Press
2 Old New Milford Road, Brookfield, Connecticut 06804

The Meredith March in Mississippi, 1966.

On a muggy June evening in 1966, Stokely Carmichael spoke to a large crowd of black people in Greenwood, Mississippi. They were all taking part in a march across the state to the capital in Jackson. The march was a peaceful demonstration, a way to focus people's attention on how blacks lived in the South.

Although many federal laws had been passed guaranteeing the civil rights of black people, they still lived very poorly in the South. In many places local officials made it almost impossible for them to vote. And in their day-to-day interactions with whites on buses and in restaurants, blacks were kept from enjoying the civil rights that had been guaranteed them.

Twenty-five-year-old Stokely Carmichael was one of the youngest leaders of the civil rights movement. He was tall and slim, with flashing eyes and a wide toothy smile. But on this June night he looked upset. Most of the other leaders spoke soothing words about showing the world—through peaceful protests—that blacks deserved civil rights. But white people, especially in the South, were slow to respond to the protests. Now Stokely Carmichael was angry. He told the crowd that it was time for blacks to stop asking for their rights and begin demanding them. "What we gonna start sayin' now is 'black power,' " he said. The crowd cheered, and Carmichael repeated the slogan again and again, "black power!" Each time he said it, the crowd shouted back, "black power!"

Stokely Carmichael's angry words struck a chord in the hearts of many black people. "Black power" became an even more popular slogan than "freedom now," the well-known words of earlier phases of the civil rights movement. The slogan showed a new way of thinking among blacks. Many were tired of asking for a place in white society and began to take pride in their own race. Soon blacks, or African Americans, as many began to call themselves, created their own flag, using the colors red, black, and green. Many stopped straightening their hair and began wearing a natural, kinky "Afro" style. They also began dressing in African shirts called dashikis. All these changes were symbols of a new feeling of pride.

The new black pride movement made many white people—and even some blacks—very uneasy. To some it seemed anti-white. They said that Stokely Carmichael, and others like him, were reckless people who would say anything to get their names in the newspapers. But the black power slogan was more than a publicity stunt. It echoed in the hearts of blacks all across the land.

Little Man

Stokely Carmichael was born on June 29, 1941, in Port of Spain, Trinidad, an island in the Caribbean Sea near the coast of Venezuela. At the time, Trinidad was part of the British Commonwealth, and its rulers were chosen by the government of Great Britain. People of many different races lived on the island, including many blacks descended from African slaves, people of European descent called Creoles, and many descendants of Asian peoples. There were fewer white British people on the island than any other type. But they had most of the power and wealth. The rest were generally poor people who worked on sugar or coffee plantations or in factories in the crowded cities.

Life was hard for the blacks and other non-British people of Trinidad. They were treated as second-class citizens by the whites. Although most blacks were poor, Stokely's father, Adolphus, was a skilled carpenter who provided a good life for his family. He built a big house for them, and they always had nice clothes and plenty to eat. As a young boy, Stokely was very generous. Many of his friends were poor, and he often sneaked food out of his house for them. But when he started giving away his clothes, his grandmother hid them.

Although the Carmichaels had a better life than most blacks in Trinidad, Stokely's parents wanted to move to the United

States. They saw it as the Promised Land. When Stokely was only three years old, his mother, Mabel, went to live with her parents in the United States. One year later, Adolphus joined her. The children would follow in time. For the moment, though, Stokely was left behind with his three sisters to live with their grandmother and two aunts.

Stokely was a handsome boy with pudgy cheeks and a cheerful look in his big round eyes. He was called Little Man by his family because he seemed wise for his age. For a child, he was very aware of politics. When he was seven, he went to the polls on election day and said he wanted to vote. One of the candidates for office, a man named Uriah Butler, had fought against British rule and had even gone to jail for his beliefs. That made him a hero in Stokely's eyes. When the poll watchers told Stokely he was too young to vote, he went home and pestered his aunt. "You must vote, you must vote!" he pleaded, until she finally did.

"Life, real life"

When Stokely was eleven, he and his sisters moved to the United States to rejoin their parents. The family settled in Harlem, a black section of New York City. Stokely was thrilled by the variety of life he found there. The streets were crowded with

shops and teeming with people, noise, and color. It was all quite different from sunny, peaceful Trinidad. To Stokely, Harlem was "life, real life."

But life was harder for the Carmichaels in the Promised Land. Instead of a big roomy house, they lived in a small, cramped apartment. Adolphus Carmichael drove a cab at night to earn extra money to put himself through school. Mabel worked as a maid.

Some years later, the family moved to a three-room apartment in a Bronx high rise. Stokely began running with a local gang, the Morris Park Avenue Dukes. Although he got into mischief, he was a good student and hoped to attend the Bronx High School of Science, one of the city's top schools. But his

9

family didn't learn about the school's entrance exam for eighth graders until after Stokely had finished that grade. Stokely chose to repeat eighth grade just so he could take the exam—which he passed with flying colors.

At the Bronx High School of Science, Stokely again did very well in his studies and read widely. He had decided to follow a pre-med program and become a doctor. But events in the United States in 1960, when he was nineteen, sharpened his interest in politics.

The civil rights movement had been making progress throughout the 1950s. Blacks and some whites demonstrated against so-called Jim Crow laws in the South, which were designed to segregate—or keep separate—blacks and whites. At that time, blacks sat in the back of buses, went to separate schools, were treated at their own hospitals, and could only drink from water fountains or use restrooms marked "Colored."

In the 1950s the civil rights movement protested Jim Crow laws, which called for separate facilities for blacks and whites.

But the restrooms set aside for blacks were seldom as nice as those for whites. Sinks and drains in their bathrooms were clogged because money wasn't spent to clean them. Their schools were shacks, with no heat or even proper books and blackboards. And not only public places were segregated. So were stores, theaters, restaurants, even whole neighborhoods.

Things began to change in the 1950s. In 1954, it became illegal for schools to be segregated by race. The Supreme Court made this decision in the famous case of *Brown* v. *Board of Education*. In 1955, Rosa Parks and the National Association for the Advancement of Colored People (NAACP) led the blacks of Montgomery, Alabama, on a boycott of that city's segregated buses. Blacks refused to ride until they were no longer forced to the back of the bus while whites sat up front. Their boycott lasted more than a year. In November 1956, the Supreme Court made segregation on buses illegal.

After the success of the Montgomery bus boycott, Dr. Martin Luther King, Jr., one of its leaders, joined with sixty other black preachers to form the Southern Christian Leadership Conference (SCLC). This group became the leading force of the civil rights movement. By 1960, some court decisions had been made and some laws were passed to correct past wrongs against blacks. But in the South, blacks were still suffering because people were not being forced to follow these new laws and court decisions.

College students sit-in at Woolworth's lunch counter in Greensboro, North Carolina, in 1960.

Some blacks decided that waiting for change wasn't enough. In February 1960, four black college students staged a sit-in at a lunch counter where blacks were not allowed to sit down. The whites who worked there asked the students to leave and refused to serve them. The students' actions were a peaceful protest, a form of civil disobedience—disobeying a bad law or practice to focus people's attention on it. It worked better than they ever dreamed.

By the end of that week, hundreds of other black students had joined the four at the counter, which was forced to close down. Soon students—black and white—were sitting-in across the South. Their actions forced local police to begin to enforce the new civil rights laws.

At first, Stokely Carmichael believed the sit-ins were just a stunt to get headlines. But when he saw television news reports showing whites cursing and spitting on the protesters, he changed his mind. He decided to join the brave protesters and took part in a sit-in himself, in Virginia, during which he was beaten by whites. The beating only made Stokely more determined than ever to get involved.

"I'm gonna tell God how you treat me"

Stokely Carmichael did so well in his studies that he was offered scholarships to several universities—including Harvard, which accepted only the best students. He refused them all. Instead, he enrolled at Howard University in Washington, D.C., an all-black school. Carmichael wanted to stay close to the civil rights movement, and at Howard he met many other students who were active in it. He also joined the Student Nonviolent Coordinating Committee (SNCC, often pronounced "snick"), a national organization of young people committed to integrating blacks into American society without violence. Young people like Stokely Carmichael were getting involved in the struggle all over the country. By the end of 1960, some 70,000 black students had taken part in peaceful protests—and 3,000 of them had been arrested for it.

Despite the risks involved, Carmichael continued to work in the movement. In 1961, he joined a dramatic protest against segregated long-distance bus travel. Although integration—the mixing of races—on buses had been ordered by the Court, blacks were still being forced to the back of the bus on long trips between different states. Since no one was enforcing the Court order, students decided to act. Calling themselves the Freedom Riders, blacks and whites rode together on buses in the South, blacks sitting in front, whites in back. At rest stops, the whites used "Colored" bathrooms, and blacks used those reserved for "Whites Only."

In Anniston, Alabama, the Freedom Riders ran into trouble. A mob of angry whites attacked them with chains, bats, and pipes as the local police stood by and watched. Later, one of the buses was firebombed, and the riders barely escaped without injury. Despite this and other attacks, the Freedom Riders rode on. Stokely was so moved by their bravery that he soon went to Jackson, Mississippi, to join them. During the trip, Carmichael and the other Freedom Riders were arrested as they entered a "white" cafeteria. They were convicted of disturbing the peace and sent to jail for sixty days.

Conditions in the jail were awful. The prisoners were given dirty mattresses and fed foul-tasting food. The guards handcuffed them, shocked them with electric cattle prods, and beat

In Anniston, Alabama, the Freedom Riders, who were staging a peaceful protest against segregation on interstate buses, were attacked by a mob of angry white people.

them. Once, when Stokely was being hurt, he began singing to his guards, "I'm gonna' tell God how you treat me," and pretty soon the other prisoners joined in, too. Their singing only made the guards more angry, but that didn't stop the Freedom Riders.

Carmichael got out of jail after serving fifty-three days, and he barely made it back to Howard for the fall term. His recent experiences had changed him deeply. He now saw that the movement was his life. He changed his course of study from pre-med to philosophy—the study of systems of ideas—explaining to his mother that he "would rather heal people before they get sick."

"I have a dream"

In 1962, Adolphus Carmichael died at the age of forty-two. Stokely Carmichael had watched how his father had struggled to make his dream of America come true. He now believed that America and its racial prejudice—all the hatred toward people of different races—had "squashed" his father.

While the civil rights movement was making progress, towns and cities in the Deep South were doing everything they could to resist the new laws to help blacks. In Birmingham, Alabama, local officials decided to close parks, schools, and libraries rather than integrate them as the law required. The SCLC decided to fight back. Beginning in March 1963, Martin Luther King, Jr., led nonviolent protest marches in Birmingham. Eventually, he and fifty other demonstrators were arrested and thrown in jail. Many of the marchers were kept in jail for so long that they lost their jobs. SCLC leaders then recruited children to march, since they didn't have jobs to lose.

On May 2, children between six and eighteen years old began marching in Birmingham. When the day was over, 959 of them had been arrested. The next day, over a thousand more children left their schools to march. The police chief, Eugene "Bull" Connor, ordered his officers to sic police dogs on the children and to spray them with fire hoses—which flowed with enough force to knock a grown man flat on his back. The young marchers were slammed into buildings and cars by the powerful spray. Americans who watched such scenes on television were shocked by the cruelty of Birmingham officials. In the end, Bull Connor's own men refused to obey their chief's orders to attack the children. Segregation in Birmingham was soon ended.

Fire hoses were aimed at demonstrators in Birmingham, Alabama, in 1963.

Martin Luther King, Jr., offered his "I have a dream" speech to a crowd of a quarter of a million people in Washington, D.C.

Later in 1963, Congress was considering a new civil rights act. Movement leaders planned a march on Washington to put pressure on the lawmakers to pass it. On August 28, more than 250,000 people showed up. Martin Luther King, Jr., delivered a famous speech to the huge crowd. "I have a dream that my four little children will one day live in a nation where they will not be judged by the color of their skin, but by the content of their character," Dr. King said.

During the march, Stokely Carmichael was attending a national student association meeting as the representative from SNCC. He knew the march would lift the spirits of followers of the movement. But he also believed that "nothing concrete would come of it," that no new laws would be passed, that whites would continue to mistreat blacks. Four weeks later, it seemed as if he was right. A bomb was thrown into a black church in Birmingham, killing four little girls.

Black Power

Carmichael graduated from Howard in 1964. He was again offered a scholarship to Harvard to continue his studies, but he turned it down. He wanted to devote his energies full-time to the movement.

A year after the March on Washington, Congress passed another civil rights act. It outlawed segregation in all public and private places. But in the Deep South, whites made it hard for blacks to register to vote or take part in politics. The Democratic Party in Mississippi wouldn't even let blacks join.

In 1964, SNCC and other groups began the Mississippi Summer Project. It was meant to help blacks register to vote and also to form a new Democratic Party that would include blacks. But at the Democratic National Convention, national party leaders decided not to allow Mississippi's black Democrats to take part. Instead, they allowed only members from the racist group—the one that kept out blacks—to represent the Democrats at the national convention.

The decision left Carmichael feeling bitter. He now thought that blacks should stop trying to integrate white power structures—such as the Democratic Party—and should organize their own. He thought blacks should form a black party to deliver black votes to black candidates for office. Then blacks would win power, and real change could come at last.

Carmichael joined a SNCC project to register blacks to vote in Alabama. White officials there had devised many unfair ways to keep blacks from voting—such as only allowing five people to register on any day, or making blacks pass impossibly hard tests in order to register. Blacks in Alabama began staging peaceful marches to protest these unfair practices. During one march, a young black man was killed by local police.

To protest the killing, black leaders staged a march from Selma to the state capital in Montgomery. The marchers were attacked by state police on horseback, who beat and gassed them. When the marchers fell, police rode over their bodies. This violent day was soon known as Bloody Sunday.

Carmichael was traveling to Alabama to join the marchers in February 1965 when he heard more horrible news. Malcolm X had been murdered in New York City. Malcolm X was a controversial black leader. Unlike King, who preached nonviolence, Malcolm X said that blacks might have to use violence—in self-defense—if whites continued to abuse them. Carmichael was beginning to think that Malcolm X's ideas made more sense than King's.

The great march from Selma to Montgomery was finally held. Although it was a success, Carmichael wasn't satisfied. He and other SNCC leaders felt that King's focus on integrating white institutions was sapping energy from work that really mattered—organizing blacks to take power themselves.

Stokely Carmichael and other SNCC leaders decided to organize blacks in Lowndes County, Alabama, a typical southern town. Eight of every ten people there were black, but whites held all the power. Not a single black was even registered to vote. Carmichael and SNCC hoped to organize the blacks of Lowndes County into an all-black political party. Malcolm X had said that blacks should control the businesses and politics of their communities. Stokely Carmichael now wanted to put those ideas into practice.

In 1965 Stokely Carmichael urged voters to register in Lowndes County.

The all-black Lowndes County Freedom Organization chose a snarling black panther as its symbol. The newspapers nicknamed them the Black Panther Party. But Lowndes County whites didn't want blacks to have any power. They fought back, threatening to harm blacks who voted for the all-black party. On election day, the all-black party got less than forty-six percent of the vote, and its candidates were defeated by whites. Still, Lowndes County blacks were better organized than ever.

Carmichael was not discouraged. In May 1966, at the age of twenty-four, he was elected the new chairman of SNCC. He promised to stop staging nonviolent protests and to place only blacks in charge of the organization. He also believed in black nationalism—that blacks should fight for their own separate nation within the United States, where they alone would hold power. Carmichael's ideas made whites nervous. But he did not think that blacks who simply wanted to build something of their own were ''anti-white.'' ''When you build your own house,'' he said, ''it doesn't mean you tear down the house across the street.''

Soon SNCC joined other civil rights groups in Mississippi on a march to protest the shooting of a young black man named

The leaders of the three most powerful civil rights groups marched arm-in-arm in Mississippi: SCLC leader Martin Luther King, Jr., CORE leader Floyd McKissick, and SNCC chairman Stokely Carmichael.

James Meredith. When the marchers reached the town of Greenwood, local police arrested Carmichael for arguing with them about where his followers could camp. After spending six hours in jail, Carmichael came out and made a speech to a crowd of some six hundred marchers and supporters. "Today's the twenty-seventh time I have been arrested," he said in an angry voice, "and I ain't goin' to jail no more." Blacks had been begging for freedom for six years, he said, and had gotten nothing. "What we gonna start sayin' now is 'black power!'" Carmichael shouted. One of his companions, Willie Ricks, leaped onto the platform and yelled, "What do you want?" The crowd's reply came back loud and clear—"BLACK POWER!"

"Black power" became the marchers' slogan for the rest of the journey across Mississippi. When the march was over, many people were nervously wondering what black power meant and what Stokely Carmichael was trying to do.

Pan-Africanism

Soon after Stokely Carmichael took over at SNCC, he pulled the organization out of the White House Conference on Civil Rights. He accused that group of ignoring the real problems of blacks. Other civil rights leaders were alarmed. Roy Wilkins, director of the NAACP, said that " 'black power' . . . can mean in the end only black death.'' Carl T. Rowan, a black writer, said ''black power'' was ''phony.'' Martin Luther King, Jr., also disagreed with Carmichael's tactics, although he still worked with SNCC.

Carmichael had hoped to make SNCC stronger. But many SNCC workers were uncomfortable with his angry position and quit the organization.

Still, the black power slogan appealed to blacks across the country. Despite years of pressure from the civil rights movement, change for blacks in America was coming very slowly. New laws guaranteeing their rights were often not obeyed. For many blacks, Carmichael's angry slogan summed up their own feelings. Symbols of black power sprouted everywhere. Young African Americans created a black power salute—a clenched fist raised above the head in greeting—which became famous in 1968 when two Olympic medal winners used it during a televised ceremony.

In 1968 Olympic medal winners Tommie Smith (center) and John Carlos raised their hands in a black power salute.

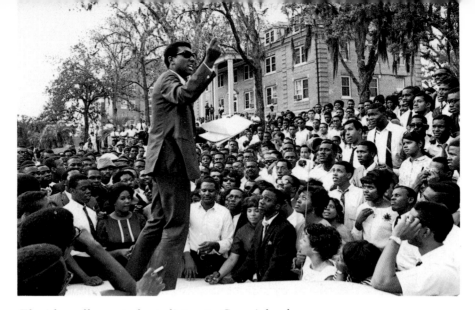

Florida college students listen to Carmichael
speak about black power in 1967.

But whites were afraid of Carmichael. The press attacked him. They said he was reckless and created trouble between blacks and whites just to get his name in the paper. Carmichael didn't think people had understood his views. In 1967, he helped write a book explaining them, *Black Power: The Politics of Liberation in America.*

Stokely Carmichael was attacked so often that he resigned as SNCC chairman in May 1967. (The organization broke up a few years later.) Carmichael began giving lectures to college students in the United States and overseas. Hours after one of his speeches, in Nashville, Tennessee, a riot broke out. Even though Carmichael was not there at the time, he was blamed for starting it.

The summers of 1966 and 1967 were hard times for America. Gone was the nonviolence of the civil rights movement. Blacks impatient with the slowness of change staged violent demonstrations. Riots rocked cities across the country as blacks set fires and looted to express their frustration. Although Carmichael was seldom on the scene, he and his thinking were often blamed for the violence.

On April 4, 1968, Martin Luther King, Jr., was killed. Again blacks rioted across the country. The violence lasted for months. Some again blamed Stokely Carmichael. He decided to move to Guinea, Africa, to carry on his work. He had married a South African pop singer, Miriam Makeba, and was now interested in Pan-Africanism—the idea that blacks everywhere in the world must unite in order to win justice.

In the summer of 1968, fires and rioting spread through black ghettos across America following the assassination of Martin Luther King, Jr.

THE BLACK PANTHERS

In 1966 black radicals in Oakland, California, led by Huey Newton and Bobby Seale, formed the Black Panther Party for Self-Defense (BPP). In many cities blacks had been beaten or even killed by the police, and the BPP wanted to protect them. The group's name came from the black panther symbol of the Lowndes County Freedom Organization.

The BPP was flashy and aggressive. Members wore black leather jackets and black berets, and they armed themselves with pistols and rifles. They often arrived at the scene of an arrest to make sure that the police behaved correctly. Their actions alarmed many people.

After Stokely Carmichael left the chairmanship of SNCC, the BPP named him "honorary Prime Minister." He was one of their spokesmen, along with others such as Eldridge Cleaver, author of the book *Soul on Ice,* which told of his experiences in the black ghetto and in prison.

The BPP ran programs that helped its community, such as providing free breakfasts for children. But even some supporters thought that the group was more of a street gang than a political party. In 1967 and 1968, many BPP leaders were arrested during heated arguments and fights with the police, and some were jailed. After that, the group faded out of sight.

Stokely Carmichael with his first wife, Miriam Makeba.

Carmichael's speeches still upset many people. The British government banned him from all of its lands. In 1978, his marriage to Makeba ended in divorce, and he married a Guinean woman, Malyatou, with whom he had a son. By now, Carmichael had also changed his name to Kwame Ture.

Many people disagreed with Stokely Carmichael's ideas. But he voiced the frustration felt by many blacks with the slow pace of change in the United States. Later black leaders took on, as Carmichael had, the job of organizing their people to vote. As a result, hundreds of black candidates have risen to local, state, and national office. Perhaps as important, by expressing his anger and his sense of injustice, Carmichael helped blacks to gain a sense of pride in themselves.

Even so, Stokely Carmichael believes that the lives of African Americans have not improved much since the sixties. He still lives in Guinea and is still working to unite people of African descent the world over.

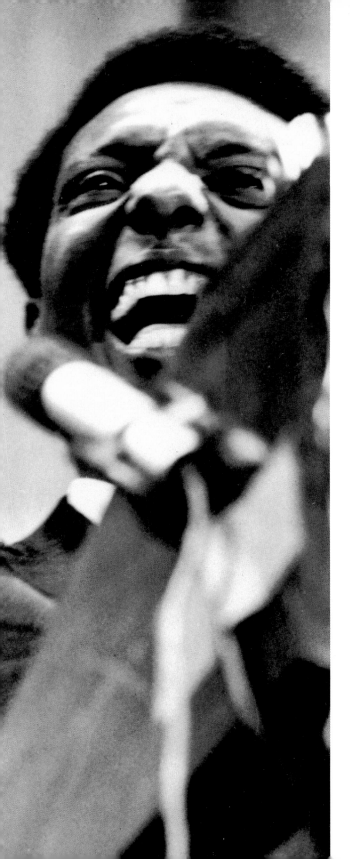

IMPORTANT DATES IN THE LIFE OF STOKELY CARMICHAEL

1941   Carmichael is born on June 29 in Port of Spain, Trinidad.

1952   Carmichael moves to Harlem in New York City.

1960   Carmichael enrolls at Howard University in Washington, D.C. He joins the Student Nonviolent Coordinating Committee.

1961   Carmichael joins the Freedom Riders in protest against segregated interstate buses.

1964   Carmichael graduates from Howard University.

1965   Carmichael helps organize blacks to vote in Lowndes County, Alabama.

1966   Carmichael is elected chairman of SNCC in May. He uses the "black power" slogan for the first time.

1967   Carmichael co-authors *Black Power: The Politics of Liberation in America*.

1968   Carmichael moves to Guinea, Africa, and changes his name to Kwame Ture.

FIND OUT MORE ABOUT
STOKELY CARMICHAEL AND HIS TIMES

The Civil Rights Movement in America from 1865 to the Present by Patricia McKissack and Fredrick McKissack (Chicago: Childrens Press, 1987).

If You Lived at the Time of Martin Luther King by Ellen Levine (New York: Scholastic, 1990).

I Have a Dream: The Life and Words of Martin Luther King, Jr. by Jim Haskins (Brookfield, Ct.: The Millbrook Press, 1992).

Malcolm X and Black Pride by Robert Cwiklik (Brookfield, Ct.: The Millbrook Press, 1991).

Martin Luther King, Jr., and the March Toward Freedom by Rita Hakim (Brookfield, Ct.: The Millbrook Press, 1991).

Stokely Carmichael: The Story of Black Power by Jacqueline Johnson (Englewood Cliffs, N.J.: Silver Burdett, 1990).

Kwame Ture at his home in Guinea, Africa, in 1978.

INDEX